Supporting Children in Public Care in Schools

Supporting Children in Public Care in Schools

A Resource for Trainers of Teachers, Carers and Social Workers

John Holland and Catherine Randerson

Jessica Kingsley Publishers
London and Philadelphia

First published in 2005
by Jessica Kingsley Publishers
116 Pentonville Road
London N1 9JB, UK
and
400 Market Street, Suite 400
Philadelphia, PA 19106, USA

www.jkp.com

Library of Congress Cataloging in Publication Data
Holland, John, 1948-
  Supporting children in public care in schools : a resource for trainers of teachers, carers and social workers / John Holland and Catherine Randerson.
    p. cm.
  ISBN-13: 978-1-84310-325-7 (pbk. : alk. paper)
  ISBN-10: 1-84310-325-7 (pbk. : alk. paper) 1. Children with social disabilities—Education. 2. Children with social disabilities—Services for. 3. School social work. I. Randerson, Catherine. II. Title.

LC4065.H65 2005
  371.826'942—dc22

                                                            2005010912

British Library Cataloguing in Publication Data
A CIP catalogue record for this book is available from the British Library

ISBN-13: 978 1 84310 325 7
ISBN-10: 1 84310 325 7

Printed and Bound in Great Britain by
Athenaeum Press, Gateshead, Tyne and Wear

Contents

Acknowledgements

The authors thank the following for their involvement and support in the development of *Supporting Children in Public Care in Schools*:

Hazel Hughes, Chris Parkinson, Peggy Devine, Judith Haldenby, Anny Bibby, Dawn O'Neil, Katherine Cawthorne, Neil Smith, Judith Dent and the staff and young people of the Young Person's Support Service (YPSS), King Edward Street, Hull as well as the teachers and carers who contributed to the preceding research project.

Preface

Supporting Children in Public Care in Schools is an awareness raising training pack for those working with children in public care, with a focus on schools. It is the latest part of a strategy involving collaborative multi-agency and multi-professional work carried out in the Hull area over several years.

Supporting Children in Public Care in Schools was developed by John Holland (of the City Psychological Service, Hull) and Catherine Randerson (of the Inter-agency Link Team, Hull). The underpinning research involved surveys of designated teachers and carers and interviews with children in public care and care leavers who had had time to reflect on their own experiences. Many of their ideas were incorporated in the training pack.

The course was developed during 2003 and 2004 and several pilot courses have been run in Hull with teachers, social workers and carers training together. The course partly uses concepts and ideas developed in the parallel *Lost for Words* training pack, published by Jessica Kingsley Publishers in 2005, which focuses on loss through bereavement.

1

Introduction

Supporting Children in Public Care in Schools is an 'awareness' training pack for use with teachers, social workers, carers and all those supporting young people who are in public care. It is underpinned by research carried out with teachers, social workers, carers and care leavers.

The aim of *Supporting Children in Public Care in Schools* is to help teachers, social workers, carers and others working with young people in public care to gain an insight into the experiences of the young people and to help to support them, especially to help ease their transitions into school.

Supporting Children in Public Care in Schools is designed for delivery to staff in schools or other settings. It comprises 'stand-alone' topic areas and facilitators can choose which topics are appropriate for their context.

We deliver *Supporting Children in Public Care in Schools* over a single day and would suggest this is the best approach although it could be delivered over two half days or several twilight sessions.

We have delivered the training in mixed groups of teachers, carers and social workers and it has been well received. The main benefit of having carers, social service staff and teachers together has been that it helps each group to develop a better understanding of the others' perspective. Professions no longer remain isolated but work in a multi-professional way for the benefit of young people. The advertising of the course needs to address all the different agencies.

The resource provides templates for overhead projector (OHP) transparencies, guidance notes for facilitators and handouts for course members. Purchasers may photocopy materials and make transparencies for OHPs as required. Kindly acknowledge the source of any materials used.

For further information, please contact:

City Psychological Service
Learning Services
Kingston upon Hull City Council
2nd Floor, Essex House, Manor Street
Kingston upon Hull HU1 1YD
Tel: 01482 613390

2

Introducing course members to the package

Planning

Ideally the course could be delivered on a training day or days, rather than in a 'twilight session' after the hustle and bustle of a busy day at work. Thought should be given to the size of the training group. Too large or too small a group may influence members' participation in activities and the sharing of experiences. A large group may inhibit members from joining in, or be dominated by individuals. An ideal group size is generally in the range of eight to sixteen members.

Consideration needs to be given to the seating arrangements. A circle or semi-circle of chairs may be better to encourage interaction rather than having the chairs in rows. It is suggested that the ground rules and ice-breaker sections are always included in any delivery to help course members to become more at ease.

Individuals may find that the course evokes difficult experiences or memories and facilitators need to give thought as to how to provide support if this is needed. Participants should be made to feel comfortable and be able to leave the room at any time; care should be taken to minimise any barriers between them and the door. A distressed participant could be asked what would help them and a facilitator or colleague may need to offer individual support.

Delivery

Facilitators should introduce themselves at the beginning of the course, explain the general purpose and aims of the course and then ask the course members to introduce themselves. The provision of handouts at the end of the course can be highlighted at this stage.

Housekeeping matters are important, so things such as toilets, canteen, heating and arrangements in case of a fire should be addressed. It is also helpful for mobile phones to be switched off at this stage.

A main aim of the course is to share and learn from the experiences of others (teachers, social workers, carers and others involved with looked-after children) so during the course members should be encouraged to split up from colleagues and change groups for different exercises. Facilitators could adopt strategies such as allocating numbers to the course members as they enter, and change the group composition as appropriate.

The 'closing down' of the course is also a very important activity, allowing the course members to disengage emotionally. It may be helpful for the facilitators to bring a session to a close by giving the course members the opportunity to share their thoughts about the session. The facilitators should wait around after the session has finished, in case there are issues that arise that course members wish to raise informally.

3
Ethos

Introduction

It is crucial that the group set some ground rules to guide the course experience. As some participants may be sensitive to course materials, the session involves some sharing of personal experience and as the group may be quite mixed in background, it is vital that members are comfortable with the arrangements.

Areas for consideration could include confidentiality within the group, 'opt-out' possibilities for individual exercise participation or at any point of the session/day, a culture of caring and respecting all contributions made and 'active listening'.

Method of delivery

The group could devise its own ethos or ground rules by brainstorming their ideas and recording them on a flip chart or whiteboard.

If the group is unsure, or if time is short, then it is suggested that the facilitators provide guidance. Transparency 1 could be used as a stimulus for a group discussion.

Whichever option is used, course members should then be invited to add any further points of their own if they wish.

The rules may be displayed throughout the course of the training as a reminder and attention could be drawn to them as appropriate, for example after breaks.

Materials

- Flip chart or whiteboard and pens
- Overhead projector (OHP)
- Transparency 1
- A copy of Transparency 1 with any additions agreed in the group and displayed, if required, throughout the training

Ethos

- Confidentiality

- 'Opt-outs'

- Caring

- Listening

4
Ice-breakers

Introduction

Ice-breakers can encourage course members to relax, talk and to engage more quickly in the training. They are particularly useful when a group consists of people from different backgrounds and also to help with the introduction of an unknown facilitator.

Aim

To help 'break the ice' between group members.

Method of delivery

A list of suggested five-minute ice-breakers follows. These could be used with the course members working together in pairs, and then some or all pairs reporting back to the whole group.

1. *Something in common with a partner*

   Ask the course members to talk with a partner they do not know, to find something that they have in common.

2. *Listening to your partner*

   Ask the course members to talk about themselves to their partner who remains silent. Ask the course members to swap their roles after two minutes.

3. *Who would you like to have a 'one to one' with?*

   Ask the course members to find out from their partner who they would like to talk with in a 'one-to-one' telephone conversation. The person could be living or dead.

4. *Films seen recently*

   Ask pairs of course members to discuss a film that they have recently enjoyed.

5. *Animal madness*

    Ask the course members to choose individually what animal they would like to be and why!

6. *Something good*

    Ask the course members to listen as a partner describes something good that has happened to him or her during that week. Ask the course members to swap roles after two minutes.

5

Identifying the training needs

Introduction

A local study, carried out by John Holland with designated teachers, carers and care leavers, set the scene for the development of the pack by identifying the training needs. These needs are outlined here: further research findings are integrated throughout the resource pack.

Supporting Children in Public Care in Schools addresses some of these training needs of designated teachers and carers. It also raises awareness through the thoughts and feelings of care leavers.

Method of delivery

Present the main study findings from the overhead transparencies, allowing time for course members to comment and raise issues. The transparencies show the training needs of both designated teachers and carers. The course members could be asked to reflect on whether they share similar views to those in the findings and whether any of the results are a surprise.

Materials

- OHP
- Transparencies 2 and 3

✓

Designated teachers' training needs

- Awareness raising for ALL staff

- Clarity of roles and responsibilities

- How to complete a Personal Education Plan (PEP)

- Awareness of attachment issues

Carers' training needs

- More information about schools

- Information about general education, especially the Code of Practice

- Better explanation of educational jargon

- Explanatory leaflets

- How to help with education, e.g. homework

6

Corporate parenting

Introduction

For young people in public care, corporate parenting involves the whole local authority and many other organisations, not just social services. We *all* have responsibility in this area. Corporate parenting gives a collective group the responsibility to do at least what good parents should do with regard to their own children. There is a need for us all to safeguard and promote the welfare of young people, as directed by the Children Act, Section 22. To do this, effective co-ordination is crucial to help to maximise the potential of young people.

The range of individuals and agencies involved in delivering corporate parenting is diverse. It includes elected members, senior officers and managers of the local education authority (LEA) and social services departments, and representatives of the health trust/authority. This is a potentially overwhelming number of professionals involved in the care of any one looked-after child.

Aim

The idea is to emphasise the concept of corporate parenting and its wide scope. The aim is also to highlight the responsibility that we all share in this area and to stress the importance of effective communication and liaison.

Method of delivery

This session could be conducted by asking the group for their thoughts on what is involved in being a corporate parent and recording this on a flip chart or whiteboard. The group could then be shown Transparency 4. Alternatively Transparency 4 can be shown and discussed with any additional contributions being recorded as appropriate on a flip chart or whiteboard. The course members can then be given Handout 1.

Materials

- Flip chart or whiteboard and pens
- OHP
- Transparency 4
- Handout 1

Corporate parenting

- Whole local authority

- Role of a 'parent'

- Welfare/safeguard

- Children Act, Section 22

- Co-ordination

Handout 1: Corporate parenting

Care, health and education are all closely linked and parents play an extremely important role in all these aspects of a young person's life, having a continuous knowledge of their children. Children in public care often do not have the benefit of such knowledge or the continuity of such care.

Corporate parenting emphasises the collective responsibility of local authorities to achieve good parenting for all young people who have been taken into public care. *A corporate parent is expected to do at least what a good parent would do.* Once a young person has been removed from his or her family then it is the duty of the *whole local authority* to 'safeguard and promote their welfare'. The 'whole local authority' includes the education department, and therefore schools also have an important part to play.

The range of individuals and agencies involved in delivering corporate parenting is diverse. It includes elected members, senior officers and managers of both the local education authority (LEA) and social services, children's services, representatives of the health trust/authority, head teachers, school governors, social workers, resident social workers and foster carers, education social workers, teachers and learning support assistants, educational psychologists and education support personnel, careers advisers, personal advisers, fostering/family placement managers and parents. There are a potentially over-whelming number of professionals involved in the care of any one child in public care.

The extent of involvement will vary greatly but it is vital that the actions and efforts of everyone involved mean that the overall corporate parenting is 'good parenting'. Lack of co-ordination may impair outcomes for young people in public care.

Expectations of an authority as a corporate parent are set out within the 'Quality Protects' framework. This is a government initiative that was launched in 1998 to improve children's services. One of the objectives was to 'ensure that children looked after gained maximum life chance benefits from educational opportunities, health care and social care'. There will also be dynamic guidance on promoting the health of looked-after children and it is important that everyone takes note of these as part of an overall strategy to improve quality of care.

Young people in public care should not be considered as a homogeneous group, because clearly there is considerable variation within the group. All those involved in corporate parenting are expected to promote achievement and actively challenge instances of less favourable or different treatment of looked-after children.

Early and appropriate intervention and action in these young people's lives is crucial and corporate parents should endeavour to take priority action to avoid disaffection and exclusion. This includes positive experiences at all levels and not necessarily referral on to specialist services.

Both the Children Act and the United Nations Convention on Human Rights state that young persons' wishes should be taken into account and there is therefore a responsibility to ascertain wishes and feelings. Good parents would carry this out and therefore 'Quality Protects' demands that local authorities listen to young people to help them plan and deliver services.

7

Why young people are in public care

Introduction

Young people come into public care for many reasons including physical or sexual abuse, domestic violence, severe neglect, or through illness or death in their family. They may be unaccompanied asylum seekers, their family may be unable to cope or there may be drug, alcohol, or substance abuse.

Most young people in care come from families experiencing difficulties and are separated from them through some form of family hardship or breakdown. Many have faced rejection, loss, change and uncertainty that would challenge adults.

Aim

The outcome of this exercise should be the realisation that young people come into public care through varied circumstances over which they have generally little or no direct control. Lack of control itself may be an issue for many young people in public care.

Method of delivery

Ask the course members to brainstorm the reasons why young people are in public care. Record their thoughts on a flip chart or whiteboard. (Transparencies 5 and 6 could be used if necessary.) Highlight the wide range of potential reasons why young people enter public care, the danger of stereotyping them as a homogeneous group, and the general lack of control that these young people have in their lives. Transparency 7 could be shown next as a summary. The course members can then be given Handout 2.

Materials

- Flip chart or whiteboard and pens
- OHP
- Transparencies 5, 6 and 7
- Handout 2

Why young people are in public care (1)

- Physical/sexual/emotional abuse

- Severe neglect

- Mental health difficulties

- Illness/death in family

- Family can't cope

- Abandonment

- Unaccompanied asylum seekers

Why young people are in public care (2)

- Drug/alcohol/substance misuse

- Domestic violence

- Homelessness

- At risk from own behaviour

- Disability of child/adult

- Imprisonment of carers

- Detention and/or training order

Why young people are in public care (3)

- Most young people in public care come from families that have experienced severe hardship or breakdown.

- Many young people in public care have faced loss, rejection, change and uncertainty that adults would find extremely difficult to cope with.

Handout 2: Why young people are in public care

Young people come into public care for a variety of reasons including physical abuse, sexual abuse, neglect, domestic violence, illness or death in the family; they may also be unaccompanied asylum seekers, their family may be unable to cope or there may be drug, alcohol or substance misuse.

Most young people in public care come from families that have experienced difficulties and they are removed as a result of some form of family hardship or breakdown. Many young people will have faced rejection, loss, change and uncertainty to a level that an adult would find hard to cope with.

The circumstances mentioned above could have been experienced in isolation but it is more likely that a number of these factors will have contributed to a young person being taken into care. This is a vast and diverse range of experiences and thoughts and emotions to have faced. Add to this that the young people may have either witnessed or been involved themselves in the situation. What is almost certain is that they will have felt *out of control* for at least part, if not all, of the time.

They may have felt out of control and affected by the situation for some considerable time before social services and the possibility of 'care' has been discussed. There may be circumstances around this that cause the young people to feel guilty and divide their loyalties between what is thought by others to be in their best interests and their natural feelings towards their families and wanting to stay with them.

Unlike a loss through bereavement a loss through going into public care may be compounded over and over. The family may still be there, be seen perhaps irregularly and all these thoughts and feelings can therefore become even more complex.

Add to the situation the different levels of understanding and different ages of young people in care and it becomes evident that all young people in the care system should be treated as individuals. They will have their own strengths and weaknesses and the fact that their life experiences have been challenging does not mean that they cannot succeed.

Young people in public care have not all experienced the same life events, nor will they cope with things in the same way. They are not a homogeneous group and should not therefore be regarded as one.

It is worth trying to consider young people's experiences through their eyes and contemplating how you would have coped in their shoes. If this then informs your practice it can only serve to help the young people with whom you work.

8

Young people in public care, attainments and attendance

Introduction

Young people in public care can tend not to perform as well academically as their peers. In terms of ability they begin as a representative sample population but their results and life chances after leaving education do not always reflect this. In some cases this may be a result of numerous factors and the lack of stability and frequent changes of school and care places may have impact, as well as emotional effects. In other cases it may be more directly related to issues of attendance. The perceptions of care leavers, designated teachers and carers are important in terms of deconstructing why this is the case. Children in public care as a group do generally value education highly.

Aim

The outcome of this exercise is for the course members to realise that young people in public care, despite being representative in terms of the general range of ability, tend to perform relatively poorly as a group. There could be many reasons why this is the case. The views of the care leavers and the perceptions of the carers and designated teachers may be important factors and hold clues to this dilemma.

Method of delivery

Present the course members with Transparency 8 showing the attainments of children in public care compared with children overall. If an explanation of Key Stages is required see Chapter 17, 'Jargon busting'. Children in public care generally underachieve through their school careers, although the vast majority consider that education is important. Ask the course members whether this comes as a surprise and their thoughts on the underlying reasons.

The figures in Transparency 8 are from the Social Inclusion Unit report *A Better Education for Children in Care*, Social Inclusion Unit 2003. There are of course significant variations: those with stable placements who have been in public care for a long time tend to do better, as do girls and children placed with their own local authority.

Show the course members Transparency 9, related to messages that leavers asked the authors to give to those on the training course. This was based on interviewing a group of leavers who had previously been in the care system. Some of the leavers' views were very forthright as to how they felt that adults had let them down, and they were clearly angry and not constructive. Ask the course members for their views on the transparency; are they surprised? If so, or if not, then why and what can be done?

Transparency 10 relates to the perceptions of designated teachers (DTs) and carers in a currently unpublished study carried out by one of the authors. The tables show the percentages of designated teachers and carers who considered that children in public care had learning or attendance difficulties. There were some interesting and at times apparently differing views. Ask for general feedback and discuss; for example, are the course members surprised by the results and what are their own experiences? Why do they think that there are differences between the views of the teachers and carers and is there a stereotypical 'child in public care'? Were the leavers right? The course members can then be given the handout.

Materials

- OHP
- Transparencies 8, 9 and 10
- Handout 3

Young people in public care and attainments

- Key Stage 2 SATs: children in public care achieve half as well as their peers

- 8% of children in public care achieved 5 GCSEs grades A–C (compared to 50% of all pupils)

- 50% of children in public care leave school with no GCSE qualifications

- 97% of children in public care rated education as important

Messages from leavers

- Don't stereotype children in public care

- Listen more, try to understand

- Some people are there for you: most are not bothered!

- I'm NOT coming back!

Children in public care and learning difficulties

	DT	Carers
Always	0%	25%
Sometimes	91%	59%
Very occasionally	9%	16%

Children in public care and attendance difficulties

	DT	Carers
Always	36%	41%
Sometimes	47%	21%
Very occasionally	17%	38%

Handout 3: Young people in public care, attainments and attendance

Young people who are in public care tend to have lower attainments than their peers, and at times their attendance can be problematic, especially at Key Stage 4; however, as a group they tend to value education.

Fifty per cent of children in public care achieved the average levels in national achievement tests at the end of Year 2 in 2002, compared with 85 per cent of the general population. This already limited academic progress declines further by Year 11 when 75 per cent of young people in care leave school with no formal qualifications at all.

In 2002, only eight per cent of young people in care achieved five GCSEs grades A–C, compared with 50 per cent of the general population. Furthermore, only 53 per cent achieved one GCSE grades A–G, compared with 95 per cent of the general population.

A further point to highlight is that the educational targets for children in public care remain much lower than those of the general population. This may be an acknowledgement of the difficulties and distractions that young people in care face, together with the limited resources of those people who try to help them. On the other hand it may be questioned why we are setting an average population of young people lower standards of achievements than their peers.

Sometimes the poorer performance of young people in care can be attributed to their lower levels of attendance at school. The statistics however do not always support this. It is important not to assume that all children in care will have poor attendance or play truant from school. What is important is that all young people are encouraged to attend as often as possible, while understanding that their whole concentration may not always be on the academic and allowances may be beneficial.

9

The experience of being in public care

Introduction

Young people who are in public care may experience a wide range of losses, beyond the obvious loss of their family. Some young people may continue to have contact with their family and perhaps experience frequent loss if this contact is erratic, which can become quite complex as their emotions may be on a 'roller coaster ride'. Young people in public care may have also experienced the loss of their pets, home, friends, school and other 'frameworks' of their life. For some the situation may be made even more complex by attachment difficulties.

Although young people should have all their physical and material needs met in public care, the context in which they find themselves may not, for lots of different reasons, meet their emotional needs. The young person may be reluctant to build relationships in a situation that may only be temporary and carers may also be reluctant to engage emotionally, for similar reasons. The young person may not receive, or even be able to accept, unconditional love or emotional support at all.

Aim

Considering the experience of loss should help the course members to gain an insight into the experiences of young people who are in public care.

Method of delivery

Show the course members Transparency 11, Angela in care, and ask them whether they have encountered similar cases in their own school or work context. Ask them to consider the potential reasons behind the presentation and discuss this for a few minutes with the person sitting next to them.

Give the course members Angela's history on Handouts 4 and 5 and ask them, in their pairs, to identify all the different losses she has experienced; these can be recorded on Handout 6. Ask the course members to report their findings to the group through brainstorming, recording the results on a flip chart. The course members can then be given Handout 7.

Materials

- OHP
- Flip chart or whiteboard and pens
- Transparency 11
- 'Angela' handouts (Handouts 4, 5 and 6)
- Handout 7

Angela in care

Angela is eleven years old and she is described by teachers as being withdrawn and showing few emotions at school. She is unable to form close relationships with her peer group or staff. Angela has occasional severe temper outbursts and is not coping academically at school. She has poor attendance and her carers say that she has disrupted sleep, nightmares, and often wets the bed.

Handout 4: Angela in care

Angela is eleven years old and is the third child of four in her family. She is the subject of a Care Order and has recently been moved into a short-term emergency foster placement for a month, after the breakdown of a long-term placement. It is hoped to find another long-term placement soon but currently one is not available. Angela has been in care twice before and has had one stay with her aunt; all were unsuccessful.

Handout 5

Angela sees her younger brother who lives nearby, but has little contact with her other brothers, one of whom is in a secure unit. Angela always seems to look forward to these visits, but then does not appear to find them a positive experience. Angela's mother is now terminally ill, and is unable to care for or cope with any of her children. Her illness follows a long history of drug abuse.

Handout 6: Angela's losses

Handout 7: The experience of being in public care

Young people in public care may experience a wide range of losses, beyond the obvious loss of their family. Some young people may continue to have contact with their family and this can lead to frequent loss experiences. The situation can become very complex as emotions may be on a 'roller coaster ride'. In addition to the loss of their family a young person in public care is also likely to have experienced other loss: for example, home, friends, pets, school, etc. If young people experience attachment disorders this may complicate the situation further.

Although young people should have all their physical and material needs met in care, the context in which they find themselves may not necessarily meet their emotional needs. This could be for many different reasons as both a carer and a young person will bring their own history and experiences to the situation. It may not be for lack of trying but for various reasons unconditional love and emotional support may not be provided or accepted at all.

A young person may be reluctant to build relationships that may only be temporary, and carers may be reluctant to engage emotionally, for similar reasons. These issues of permanence and stability in the new relationships can cause pressure. Time will be required to adjust and build trust between people. Sometimes this is not possible owing to the chaos and speed that may surround a move.

Problems may arise with the planning of moves, the sharing of information, the time scales and the expectations of those involved. A young person may feel out of control and feel his or her opinions are not important.

Experiences in children's homes can be particularly difficult owing to an unavoidable lack of continuity of care. Here young people have to adjust to a series of carers, not just one or two. This may involve different personalities and approaches to care and can confuse and upset a young person even more. Added to this is the fact that a number of young people will be living at the residence. Even once a young person is no longer the 'new arrival', these arrangements can cause social issues.

The whole experience of being in care can involve lots of loss. Always consider the impact of this on a young person's behaviour and mental health.

10

Loss experience

Introduction

There is a wide range of losses that can affect us and have an emotional impact. Individuals may find the subject of loss difficult and may not connect the 'theory of loss' with their own personal experiences. Loss is on a continuum from small to great and this section of the course is intended to engage participants in considering a loss experience other than the breaking of a bond with a person through an event such as death or rejection. The range of emotions experienced may be quite similar for small losses and can then be transferred into thoughts of other losses at a more intense level. The section does refer in broad terms to some models of loss that have been used to help conceptualise the experience of loss: this provides a framework to help understand but does not imply that those not going through the experience in a particular way are 'ill'.

Aim

Consideration of the loss experience, in this context, may help course members to consider the area of loss in a non-threatening way and, at the same time, give them an insight into the range of emotions that may be involved in different types of loss experience that will give them empathy with the loss experiences of children in public care.

Method of delivery

Display and discuss Transparency 12, which shows some of the wide range of losses that could be experienced, stressing that there is no hierarchy of losses; they cannot be compared in terms of the effect on the individual.

Ask the course members either in pairs or small groups to consider one of the situations in Handout 8. The handout can be cut into sections for the purpose of this group work. The situations are:

- losing a favourite thing

- moving to a new house in a new area

- your best friend moving a long way away

- your favourite sports team being relegated from a league.

Ask the course members to spend a few minutes imagining how they would feel at the following time periods:

- at the time of the loss

- after two weeks

- after six months

- after two years.

Show the course members Transparency 13 to remind them of the time periods. Ask the course members in pairs or small groups to discuss *their own* likely feelings at the various times shown and then to report these back to the group.

Transparency 14 may then be used to show the course members the wide range of potential emotions felt after a loss. The point could then be made that there are many shared and similar feelings after any loss.

The final part of this section is optional and may be used if appropriate for course members.

Transparency 15 shows three examples of models of loss. Models of loss give some structure to the emotional response after a loss, but they are *not* prescriptive as people vary in terms of their response.

Transparencies 16, 17 and 18 summarise the main components of the three models mentioned, the 'passive', 'active' and 'continuing bonds' models. Put simply, the 'passive' model tends to show individuals going through loss and experiencing emotions in stages, the 'active' model tends to perceive the experience as individuals having tasks to achieve, and the 'continuing bonds' model sees loss as more woven into life stories and experiences. The course members could be shown the transparencies and referred to the handouts and further reading for a more detailed understanding of loss.

Materials

- Flip chart or whiteboard and pens

- OHP

- Transparencies 12 to 18

- Handout 8

- Handout 9

Losses

- Pet
- Friendship
- Marriage
- Home
- Security
- Sense of belonging
- Parent
- Starting/leaving school/college/class
- Community
- Innocence
- Faith/religion
- Possessions
- Freedom
- Loss through divorce/separation

- Children
- Limb
- Work (through retirement/ redundancy)
- Loss through birth/ death of sibling
- Relationships
- Stability
- Sense of self-worth
- Physical/mental health
- Dreams
- Loss through emigration
- Culture

How would you feel?

- At the time of loss

- After two weeks

- After six months

- After two years

Loss feelings

- Anger
- Blame
- Guilt
- Shock
- Confusion
- Relief
- Horror
- Disbelief
- Sadness
- Being upset
- Regret
- Worry

- Preoccupation
- Resignation
- Fear
- Unhappiness
- Panic
- Disappointment
- Anxiety
- Distress
- Yearning
- Frustration
- Depression
- Abandonment

Models of loss

- Passive model

- Active model

- Continuing bonds model

Passive model of loss (stage based)

- Shock and denial

- Separation and pain

- Guilt and anger

- Sadness

- Resolution

Active model of loss (task based)

- Accept the reality

- Feel the pain

- Adjust to the loss

- Invest emotional energy elsewhere

Continuing bonds model of loss

- A continuing relationship

- No 'detachment'

- Changing but continuing relationship

- No 'resolution'

Handout 8: Losses

- Losing a favourite thing

- Moving to a new house in a new area

- Your best friend moving a long way away

- Your favourite sports team being relegated from a league

Handout 9: Loss experience

Loss can potentially be a difficult and emotive subject and we may not connect the 'theory' with our own personal experiences. Loss is on a continuum from small to great and considering the smaller loss of an object, rather than a significant loss, can help to understand the feelings that are associated with greater losses. The range of emotions experienced may well be similar whatever the loss but the intensity is likely to be different.

Loss can be difficult, especially when connected with the loss of an individual, whether through some form of separation or through death. The losses of children who are in public care may easily be overlooked or the significance of the losses minimised, yet these young people will have experienced at least one but probably a number of losses and rejections, and therefore will have experienced the associated emotions.

The experience of loss generates many feelings; sadness will not be the only emotion that is experienced when we are separated from or lose something significant in our life. Other feelings may include: anger, blame, guilt, shock, confusion, relief, horror, disbelief, anxiety, depression, frustration, distress, worry, shame, fright and abandonment.

Since loss experiences occur on a continuum there are no definitive hierarchies involved. It is not 'worse' to lose one thing rather than another. The feelings experienced will always depend on the individual and also on the degree of attachment to the thing or person who has been lost.

It may help if feelings are expressed, although not everybody finds this an easy thing to do. There may not always be the family or community support systems that are appropriate to support individuals in sharing their experiences and expressing their feelings.

If consideration is made of all the reasons causing young people to be taken into care, then an awareness of all the losses that are involved can begin. If this then proceeds to consideration of all the natural responses to losses we can begin to understand the difficulties that face young people in care and therefore the challenging behaviour and anomalies of learning that sometimes face us.

The findings upon which this course has been partly based suggest that we should give more consideration to approaching these young people as individuals, rather than as 'children in public care'. We need to consider their losses as real and to acknowledge the subsequent feelings about their experience; these may well be ongoing and not settled.

Models have been devised to help explain and understand loss as an experience. The following is a simple view; for a more complex perspective the reader's attention is drawn to the significant amount of literature available in this area.

There is no shared hierarchy of loss and for each individual the experience will depend on the degree of attachment and how the loss or losses are perceived by the young person. The losses of young people in public care are rarely straightforward, are frequently complex and the better that they are considered and understood, the better we can begin to help and support the young people.

Humans are essentially social animals, despite the odd 'hermit', and the making of these social bonds helps to promote group cohesion. When these bonds are broken, individuals may have a grief reaction, the degree of which depends on the context and the significance of the loss. Models should be seen as 'pegs' on which to hang concepts and experiences and not as definitive.

According to Kübler-Ross (1970) a person who has experienced a loss may pass through a series of stages. Individuals are often in a state of *shock* after experiencing a loss and they may also *deny* that the event has happened. Feelings of *separation and pain* may naturally follow as the reality of the loss is realised. There may also be feelings of *guilt*, for example blaming oneself for an act or omission that might have altered the course of events or even prevented or caused the loss. There may be regrets, and anger towards oneself and others involved, for example, social services. In time anger may be replaced with feelings of *sadness* or even depression. Eventually, the loss may finally be *accepted* or *resolved*. Young people in public care may, however, have experienced more than a single loss and so they may become 'stuck' at a particular point and need significant help from others involved. In a minority of cases the support of outside agencies may be necessary.

There are various other ways of looking at loss, including the active or task model and continuing bonds model.

After a loss the first task is for the individual to *accept the reality of the loss*, and young people may be quite resilient. Work on 'wishes and feelings' may help in this adjustment. Individuals may well go through *feelings of pain and separation after a loss* and this is normal. Eventually they are likely to *adjust to the loss* in their life and finally *invest their emotional energy elsewhere*, within their new situation.

The idea of 'resolution', 'detachment' or the severing of links as being either healthy or necessary to 'move on' is a relatively contemporary notion that has been challenged and presented in models such as the continuing bonds model.

11
Attachment

Introduction

Attachment theory is helpful in terms of maintaining a focus on the needs of children in public care. Attachment is a biologically based strategy that provides emotional and physical protection for children. Attachment is the bond that develops between the baby and a significant other, usually the main carer. Attachment relationships usually begin at birth and are established by the age of eighteen months. The quality of these early attachments is thought to be quite likely to impact on the individual's future self-concept and on his or her future relationships with others.

Aim

The aim is to provide course members with an insight into some of the factors that can affect attachment in general and children in public care in particular. Although these are issues that could affect all children, they may particularly have an impact on those in public care in terms of their self-concept and future relationships, bearing in mind that their own experiences may have been more profound.

Method of delivery

Ask the course members to brainstorm ideas about the factors and experiences that may impact on the quality of a child's attachment. Record the findings on a flip chart/whiteboard and ask the group whether the responses are familiar in relation to a previous session in the course. The responses of the group may actually mirror the reasons young people are in public care.

Then show the group Transparency 19, which shows a wide range of issues that may affect attachment but that rarely occur in isolation. Although attachment relates to the initial bonding after birth between the child and the primary caregiver, it also relates to the ability to make and maintain other attachments in subsequent relationships. Ask the group for their own reflections on both the exercise and on Transparency 19. The course members can then be given the handout.

Materials

- Flip chart or whiteboard and pens
- OHP
- Transparency 19
- Handout 10

Factors potentially affecting attachment

- Physical, sexual, or emotional abuse

- Severe neglect or rejection

- Domestic violence

- Gender of the child

- Significant illness or death in the family

- Family unable to cope

- Difficult labour

- Separation from the primary carers

- Drugs, alcohol or substance abuse

- Unwanted or difficult pregnancy

- Confusing messages

- Postnatal depression

- Inconsistent or poor parenting

Handout 10: Attachment

Attachment is a biologically based theory that is useful for those working with young people in order to maintain a focus on young people's needs. Attachment is the bond that develops between the baby and a significant other, usually the main carer. Attachment relationships generally begin at birth and are established by the age of 18 months. Both secure and insecure attachments at this stage will impact on both the individual's self-concept and on his or her future relationships.

An attachment is indicated when a baby is not afraid of the attachment figure, usually the primary caregiver, but could appear afraid of others. An attachment is also likely to mean a child becomes upset when the attachment figure is not available.

An attachment should provide physical needs, safety and protection, socialisation, stimulation and allow the development of a sense of self. A strong attachment will allow a young person to develop intellectually, emotionally and socially.

Many of the factors that result in young people being taken into public care are likely to have had an influence on the quality of their primary attachment, if there were issues at the attachment-forming stage. For example abuse, neglect, illness, death, substance abuse and other problems may all act as barriers to attachment. They should not, however, be assumed definitely to lead to a poor attachment.

An abusive relationship may be the only kind of relationship that a young person understands. Although the relationship may be painful it is also familiar and most young people will prefer the security of misery to the misery of insecurity. Young children will tend to find fault with themselves rather than an adult and will feel responsible for the events. Abusive attention may be the only kind of attention available and may be perceived as better than none. There may be times when an abusive caregiver will behave in a loving way towards the young person, which may be when attachments are formed. These may also be the times that a young person remembers most, blocking out the more negative memories.

In addition to the effects of primary attachments there are likely to be added complexities for young people in public care concerning the additional attachments that are formed throughout life. Although different from primary attachments as a baby, these can still have significant effects on the forming of self-concept and future relationships.

Young people in public care may have the experience of several losses of significant others in their lives. This may have the effect of making the young person reluctant to trust or become close to anyone for fear that they too will be lost. There may be many consequences of attachment experiences that influence a young person's cognition, emotions and sociability.

12

Changes in learning and behaviour

Introduction

Changes in learning and behaviour occur for numerous reasons; one such factor may be loss. This section considers how changes in behaviour could be the expression of a range of emotions experienced by a young person after a loss. For example, a pupil presenting with behaviour difficulties may be going through the reaction of anger. A pupil whose attainments decline may actually be preoccupied with their loss and find concentration difficult.

Individuals *may* display emotional, physical, academic and social markers of their emotions. Some young people, however, may not experience any such difficulties at all.

Aim

The outcome of this exercise should be the realisation by the course members that, although there are potentially many causes of changes in behaviour and learning, a change in the behaviour of a child in public care may be a direct or indirect result of their loss. There is not, however, necessarily a causal connection as many young people who have experienced significant losses may not have such reactions.

Method of delivery

Present the study findings on Transparencies 20 and 21 which show the views of some care leavers and their reflections on their school difficulties. The group may be asked for any comments which can then be discussed. The same can be done for Transparency 22, showing the views of designated teachers and carers regarding behavioural problems. It may be interesting to raise the differences between the teachers and carers as an issue for discussion.

Small groups of course members should then be asked to consider the potential effects on learning and/or behaviour that a loss may have on pupils. Participants should be reminded of their own previous loss experiences and also of the models of loss, and that many of the effects will relate to the emotions and feelings being experienced after a loss. Ask the different groups to consider the potential difficulties under the following headings:

- emotional markers

- physical markers

- academic markers

- social markers.

Examples could be given and the course members asked to record their thoughts on flip chart paper.

After five minutes, bring the groups together and ask them to provide feedback on their conclusions. Transparencies 23 to 26 (27 where appropriate) may be used if necessary.

Highlight to course members the idea that most pupils will not need specialist input, especially if they are provided with initial and effective support. A small percentage of pupils may need to be referred elsewhere. Highlight that this is not an inevitable outcome, but that some young people did have quite negative experiences, although for others there was not the same level of difficulties. In addition, many children not in public care will experience similar difficulties. The course members can then be given the handout.

Materials

- Flip chart or whiteboard and pens

- Flip chart paper

- OHP

- Transparencies 20–26 (27 as appropriate)

- Handout 11

How some children in public care experienced difficulties at school

- Behaviour affected

- Education disrupted

- Missed exams

- Learning difficulties unrecognised or exaggerated

- Stereotyped

Care leavers said that difficulties at school led to other problems

- Solvent abuse

- Drugs

- Pregnancy

- Living on the streets

Do children in public care have behaviour problems?

	DT	Carers
Always	11%	30%
Sometimes	80%	61%
Very occasionally	9%	9%

Emotional markers

- Mood swings

- Anger

- Withdrawal

- Forgetfulness

- Depression

- Aggression

- Low self-esteem/confidence

- Regression

- Unpredictability

- Being clingy

- Violence

- Attention/approval-seeking behaviour

Physical markers

- Sleep problems (nightmares/terrors)
- Eating disorders
- Self-neglect/harm
- Headaches
- Poor sexual health
- Skin problems
- Ticks
- Hair loss
- Developmental delay
- Stomach/bowel problems
- Psychosomatic illnesses
- Vulnerability to accidents
- Bedwetting
- Poor immune system
- Dental/medical problems

Academic markers

- Poor concentration
- Withdrawal
- Low self-esteem
- Restlessness
- Disruptive behaviour
- Poor punctuality
- Needs support
- Truanting
- Lowered expectations
- Change in attainments/relationships
- Disorganisation
- Loss of interest
- School refusal
- Low confidence

Social markers

- Substance abuse
- Isolation
- Over familiarity with strangers
- Promiscuity
- Poor boundaries
- Criminality
- Arson
- Violence
- Disruptiveness/destructiveness
- Self-neglect
- Depression
- Lack of conscience/empathy
- Gambling
- Prostitution
- Vulnerability
- Suicide

Social markers (asylum seekers)

- Cultural confusion

- Community isolation

- Language difficulties

- Violence

- Withdrawal

- Racial abuse

- Friendship difficulties

- Effects of trauma

Handout 11: Changes in learning and behaviour

Changes in a young person's behaviour may be an expression of the range of emotions being experienced by them after a loss. Most young people will eventually work through these feelings in socially acceptable ways, although some may become involved in antisocial behaviour such as crime or substance abuse. The majority of young people will not need referring for specialist help; they are however likely to need time, space and support from the adults in their lives to help them through this period.

There will be variations in the length of time that young people will be affected by their loss; this depends on factors such as the context of the loss and also on the degree of their attachment. There may well be peaks and troughs of emotions, as individuals work through the issues and emotions involved.

Loss is an essentially individual experience and assumptions cannot be made about the degree to which it will affect different people. The death of a pet, for example, may be a major and significant loss for an individual. A young person may outwardly appear to be coping or unmoved, but this may not reflect their true internal state and feelings.

Individuals may act out of character at a time of loss. There may be loss of self-esteem, disturbed sleep patterns and a susceptibility to illness and minor accidents through concentration loss. Some individuals may revert to an earlier developmental stage, for example, sucking their thumbs or bedwetting.

Academic performance may be affected, either by decline, or less commonly by improvement. Young people may 'throw themselves' with enthusiasm into academic work as a way of coping with or escaping from their loss.

Behaviour changes may present over a period of time, even years after the loss event. They may also occur sporadically and resurface particularly at sensitive times like birthdays and anniversaries. Teachers and other adults at school may need to be made aware of individual circumstances. Most students will not need specialist help, but a small percentage may need to be referred elsewhere.

13

Young people as individuals

Introduction

It is important to consider the needs of all young people, especially those in public care, and how their experiences may impact on the many aspects of school life including behaviour, learning and attendance. Young people are individuals, and consideration needs to be given to individual differences of both an environmental and genetic type. These can include:

- the age of the young person
- his or her cognitive ability
- his or her personality
- the context of the loss
- the degree of attachment
- peaks and troughs in the intensity of grief
- individual experiences and construction of the loss.

It is also necessary to consider that young people often lack:

- information about what is happening
- control over events
- understanding about what is happening.

Aim

The outcome of this exercise should be a greater awareness of how individual differences and contexts impact on young people. There are important additional factors for children in public care. Information about and control over events may be very significant.

Method of delivery

Show the course members Transparency 28 and outline the individual differences that should be considered. SEN stands for special educational needs and ASD stands for autistic spectrum disorder.

The age of the young person is important, not only in terms of what they can comprehend, but also in terms of the explanations that can be made to them. Cognitive ability will also impact on how explanations can be made. The personality of the young person also needs to be taken into account.

Show the course members Transparency 29 whilst explaining that young people experience circumstances differently from adults in terms of the information that they have about what is happening and the control that they have over unfolding events. Children vary according to their previous experience of life events and the context of the loss.

Discuss any differences within the course members' experiences and opinions and talk through these points. The course members can then be given the handout.

Materials

- Flip chart or whiteboard and pens
- OHP
- Transparencies 28 and 29
- Handout 12

Young people as individuals (1)

- Age

- Cognitive ability

- SEN/ASD

- Personality

- Attachment

- Individual construction

Young people as individuals (2)

- Information

- Control

- Experience

- Context

Handout 12: Young people as individuals

In order to be able to help young people in public care we need to understand and to give consideration to the individuality of the person and their experiences. Each case will be unique and it is important to resist the tendency to stereotype children in public care.

The *age and cognitive ability* of the young person will be relevant to their experience. Young children may not be able to understand the long-term implications of their loss. It is necessary to keep explanations as clear as possible and to avoid euphemistic comments that may be taken literally. The truth is important in terms of what the young person can understand, as hiding it and trying to 'protect' young people may lead to them building fantasies that could be worse than the truth.

As children grow older their understanding increases and they may feel responsible for the loss that has occurred. It is important to reassure such children that the situation was not caused by them. Whilst taking care not to blame the adults concerned it is necessary to remove responsibility from the young person.

Older children or adolescents may have a clearer understanding of the situation and are likely to feel quite powerless as situations around them change. They may still feel responsible for the events that have occurred as they try subconsciously to find their own identity; an adolescent especially may experience many difficulties.

It is also necessary to take into account whether a young person has any special educational needs, or autistic spectrum disorder, as this too will impact on the effect of the young person's experiences. Similarly, their personality may predispose them to more stress reaction, or on the other hand increase their resilience. Attachments are also likely to have an impact; it is difficult, however, with all of these factors to theorise more specifically what this impact will be. An awareness of the possibilities is, however, important.

The *context of the loss* and *degree of attachment* is also a significant consideration. Assumptions about these should not be made. Our thoughts about the adults concerned may not be the same as the young people's; it is false to assume, if they have been hurt in any way by their carers, that they will automatically bear malice towards them. It is important to consider the sentiments the young person is expressing (both verbally and otherwise) about their loss in order to appreciate its significance to them.

Young people may experience *peaks and troughs* in their emotions about their experience. It may be wrong to assume that since they seem to be adjusting well to their new circumstances this will continue to be the case. As with any loss the grief process is a complex one and individuals may well not travel through the 'stages' of grief in sequence. Always remain aware of a young person's experiences; significant birthdays and anniversaries may occur without your knowledge; do not assume that the person has simply got out of bed on the wrong side or is trying to make your life difficult.

Each individual will have had different experiences and will construct their own loss. Some time should be taken to consider what this experience means for the individual concerned and resist the tendency to make judgements or to stereotype.

In trying to help young people in public care it is also necessary to consider that they may have *limited knowledge* or *understanding* about what is happening around them. They may feel a *lack of control* over events. These factors will further influence their experience and should be considered at all times.

14

School transitions and ongoing support

Introduction

Young people in care may well have experienced significant and numerous changes in their lives. Much of the time the changes around their personal circumstances will be chaotic and appear unplanned. There is a chance to make any necessary school transitions work much better and therefore provide one element of a young person's life with some stability, and also many general things can be done to support children in public care. Young people may not always change school after coming into public care but they will still need similar support.

Aim

The outcome of this exercise should be the realisation that the initial transition of joining a school is a key event for a young person and that it is important that it is carefully planned. In addition that there is a wide range of practical, environmental and communication strategies that can facilitate positive initial and subsequent experiences for children in public care in the medium and longer term. The exercise also gives the opportunity for course members to exchange ideas of good practice.

Main points for the facilitator to emphasise are:

- *Securing a speedy full-time educational placement* – in a local mainstream school, without delay. A maximum of twenty school days should secure an admission; a protocol for sharing information is also necessary.

- *Key people* – usually this is the designated teacher but be open to other suggestions where appropriate to make and keep contact with key people caring for the young person.

- *Acknowledgement and space to talk* – this should be considered bearing in mind the wishes of the young person, including not wishing to talk or being selective about whom they talk with.

- *Communication within school and with carers* – this needs to be quickly established and regular contact maintained. Decide how staff will be kept up to date about the young person's circumstances, and how much information is shared bearing in mind the wishes of the young person.

Most young people, given sensitive support from home and school, will not need a specialist referral. In a few cases, as mentioned in the previous section on changes in behaviour and learning, it may be necessary to seek further specialist help.

Method of delivery

Present and discuss Transparency 30. This highlights the importance of transitions for children in public care. Evidence from the study showed that 76 per cent of designated teachers and 82 per cent of carers felt that the transition stage was very important. Ask the group if this reflects their own thoughts, views and experiences.

Show the group Transparency 31 which lists the feelings that designated teachers and carers thought children in public care felt when joining a new school. Ask the group whether this reflects their own thoughts, views and experiences and whether they are surprised at the differences between the two groups, these being mainly concerned with the fact that carers felt that young people would be excited by the prospect of moving to a new school.

Divide the course members into three groups and ask them to consider one of the following issues in connection with the transition of a young person into the school:

- practical ideas to support a young person

- how to promote a positive welcoming ethos

- how to develop effective communication within the school and with outside agencies.

Bring the group back together and ask them to present their ideas to the group for general discussion. Transparencies 32 to 37 relate to the exercise and could be used to expand the discussion as well as providing a prompt for suggestions if appropriate. The course members can then be given the handout.

Materials

- Flip chart or whiteboard and pens
- OHP
- Transparencies 30 to 37
- Handout 13

How important are transitions for children in public care?

	DTs	Carers
Very important	76%	82%
Important	24%	18%

Rate the importance of transitions as a percentage

Children in public care	70%

How do children in public care feel when they move to a new school according to DTs and carers?

- Anxious

- Scared

- Vulnerable

- Disorientated

- Unsure

- Isolated

- Excited

Practical ideas (1)

- Prompt admission or reintegration

- Introductory visits to school

- Flexible timetable

- Buddy system

- Circle of friends

- Peer support

- Referral to specialist services

✓

Practical ideas (2)

- Cover story

- Induction pack

- Extra help if needed

- DT co-ordinates

- Priority action if appropriate

- Regular attendance

Ethos (1)

- Whole school approach

- Chance to be heard

- Sensitive and planned approach

- Pupil's pace

- Being honest and open

- Being positive: friendly and welcoming

- Avoiding exclusions

Ethos (2)

- Opportunity for high attainments

- Sharing of information on a 'need to know' basis

- Discussion of practical issues, e.g. uniform

- Discussion of possible triggers to adverse behaviour

- Anti-bullying strategies

Communication (1)

- Links with carers

- Links with agencies

- Links within the school

- Key person

- Designated teacher

- Continuity of key people

- Accurate records

- Involvement of former and future staff

Communication (2)

- Being open to different methods, e.g. e-mail/text

- Brief weekly contact with home

- Positives as well as negatives

- Use of induction materials

- Use of mentors

- Clarity of negotiated rules and rewards

- Good administrative support

Handout 13: School transitions and ongoing support

Young people in public care are likely to have experienced significant and numerous changes in their lives. Much of the time the changes around their personal circumstances could be chaotic and appear unplanned. There is a chance to make any necessary school transitions work better and to provide one element of a young person's life with some stability as well as doing the many general things that can support children in public care.

The transition of a young person into the school needs to be sensitively and carefully planned, as it is likely for many reasons to be a difficult time. The main issues may revolve around gaining a speedy placement, appointing key persons, acknowledging a young person's circumstance and experience as well as communicating effectively within school and with others caring for the young person.

Practical things that can be done to help with the transition include a prompt admission or reintegration into school to try to allow some consistency in at least one area of the young person's life. For similar reasons regular attendance should be promoted.

Flexible timetables, buddy systems, circle of friends, or peer support programmes are all options that might be considered to assist a transition and help children in public care in school. Other possibilities are induction packs, easy access to designated teachers and priority action and referrals if appropriate.

Outside agencies may be able to support young people and their families, although most, given sensitive support from home and school, may not need further referral. In some cases, specialist help should be accessed. This could be the case when a young person has experienced trauma or violence, when they have become depressed, or if anger is extreme or protracted. Wherever there seems to be a significant and adverse effect on the pupil's life concern should be expressed.

A whole school *ethos* should be promoted when it comes to dealing with young people in care. A sensitive and planned individual approach should always be established at the pupil's pace. Every opportunity should be given for the young person to achieve, and exclusions should be avoided as much as possible. It is important to be as honest as is possible to prevent false beliefs and hopes about the future developing, again with the help of the other agencies involved.

Individuals should not be pressed to talk, but should be given the opportunity to talk to a staff member if they so wish. Pupils may welcome space to talk, but the wishes of those who do not want to talk, or who are selective about whom they talk with, should be respected. It is important that a subject is never forced on a child in public care and that he or she is allowed to take the initiative.

Effective *communication* is vital and links to the parents or to the carers need to be very quickly established, ideally co-ordinated through the designated teacher, with regular contact then being maintained. Carers may appreciate help and advice at this early time. As much continuity of key people as possible should be achieved with effective liaison between former and future staff, accurate records being essential.

Links within school itself are important and efforts should be made to ensure that everyone who may be involved with a young person is aware of present and changing circumstances. Initially a young person may prefer to have a cover story to help explain their circumstances to their peers.

Practical issues should be discussed as much as possible with young people to try to reduce potential triggers to adverse behaviour.

15

The designated teacher

Introduction

The designated teacher has overall responsibility for young people who are in public care. They play a potentially key role in supporting children in public care in school. Each school should have one and their role might include:

- liaising with social services departments (SSD) and other agencies, both in relation to the initial transition into the school and then in continued communication

- promoting inclusive policies and robust pastoral systems in school

- encouraging clear lines of communication both with other agencies and within school

- building links with parents and carers and helping to promote active and updated Personal Education Plans (PEPs) and home–school agreements

- helping to promote a climate of high expectations of attainment and behaviour

- being aware of the difficulties that may be influencing a young person and responding and intervening as appropriate

- maintaining and sharing relevant information sensitively about individuals

- acting as a resource for staff and pupils.

Aim

The outcome of this exercise should be the realisation of the potentially wide role of the designated teacher in school. There may be interesting differences in practice between schools. It would be helpful for other practitioners to have a greater understanding of this role.

Method of delivery

Show the course members Transparency 38 and discuss any issues or additions to the list. Does the list make sense to the course members in terms of their own experiences?

Then show the course members Transparency 39 which highlights the findings from unpublished research carried out by one of the authors. Do the difficulties make sense in terms of their experiences and how could things be improved?

It may also be necessary to discuss the issue of responsibility without power in relation to the post of designated teachers as this may have been an issue for some course members. The course members can then be given the handout.

Materials

- Flip chart or whiteboard and pens
- OHP
- Transparencies 38 and 39
- Handout 14

The designated teacher

- Has key role/co-ordinator

- Liaises with family/others

- Promotes policy and systems

- Is involved in strategies

- Encourages communication

- Builds links

- Raises awareness

- Maintains records/info (PEPs)

- Controls admissions/
  re-admissions

DTs: difficulties

- Contacting social workers and carers

- Late PEPs and reviews

- Inter-agency (mis)understandings

- Lack of information transfer

- Change of placements

Handout 14: The designated teacher

The designated teacher has overall responsibility for young people who are in public care. The designated teacher has a potentially wide role to play that can support young people placed in public care in their school life. This is important because school may be the only reliable and consistent part of their experience.

- Liaising with social services departments and the other agencies that are involved, both in relation to the initial transition into the school and then in continued communication, is crucial. It is important that everyone involved is aware of the present and changing situations in order to try to understand a young person's experiences.

- Acting to promote inclusive policies and robust pastoral systems are important in terms of promoting a whole school ethos that is supportive to young people. It is not something that a regular school week may allow time for but is nevertheless something that should be aspired to in order to support practice.

- Encouraging clear lines of communication both with other agencies and within school can be an arduous task. Systems may help with this, together with delegation and the effective use of support staff.

- Links with parents or carers are very important and can help to ensure that PEPs are up-to-date and home–school agreements are kept. Generally parents or carers know their children or wards better than anyone and regular liaison can assist in information sharing and avoid damaging misunderstandings.

- Any help in promoting a climate of high expectations of attainment and behaviour for young people in public care is worthwhile. Knowledge and awareness raising is vital to this cause.

- Awareness of the difficulties that may be influencing a young person's attainments or behaviour can help staff adapt to make the school experience a positive one for children in public care as well as trying to avoid exclusions and disaffection as much as possible.

- Maintaining and sharing relevant information about individuals in a sensitive way will promote positive relationships and provide a foundation for a positive school experience for all concerned.

- Acting as a resource for staff and pupils will help everyone.

16

Personal Education Plans (PEPs)

Introduction

A PEP is a plan which is required at school for every child in public care. It includes information and plans relating to a young person's attainments and progress.

A well-established PEP assists in maximising a young person's attainments through ensuring access to services and support and regular communication between the agencies involved, as well as minimising school disruption and establishing clear goals and providing a relevant record of progress and achievement.

Aim

The outcome of this exercise is that course members acknowledge the key role of a PEP as a process and as a tool to help maximise the attainment of young people in public care.

Method of delivery

Show the course members Transparency 40 and discuss any issues or matters arising; for example, do people feel that this reflects their own experience of PEPs? If not, how could this be improved? There may be other views that course members wish to add to the list.

Split the course into groups of five and provide them with the appropriate individual 'Angela in care' role cards. Avoid allocating a role to somebody who already performs that role. Show the course members Transparency 41. Ask the groups each to hold a pre-PEP meeting to discuss Angela's start at her new school. Show Transparency 42 to remind the groups who is present at the meeting.

After about ten minutes bring the course members back together and discuss their experiences. Ask the course members to share their experiences of the role play, such as how they felt and what the issues were. Provide the opportunity for course members to 'de-role', for example, doing a round where they outline their real names and roles and what they will be doing later. The course members can then be given the handout.

Materials

- OHP
- Transparencies 40 to 42
- 'Angela in care' role cards 1 and 2, each cut into individual roles
- Handout 15

✓

Personal Education Plans (PEPs)

- Process and tool to maximise attainment

- Ensures access to services and support

- Minimises school disruption

- Establishes clear goals

- Records progress and achievement

Angela in care

Angela has moved to another foster carer and a PEP meeting has been called. Angela attends the meeting together with her mentor, social worker, current carer and designated teacher. The roles of each are outlined on the cards.

Angela

- Social worker

- Designated teacher

- Carer

- Mentor

Angela

Think about how it feels to be sat with all these people talking about you. Consider what you might want or not want. Imagine what your attitude might be, given all the experiences that you have been through. How much information would you want to give to the meeting?

Social worker

You are just beginning to build up some trust with Angela. You are concerned about the conflicts that might occur in the meeting and hope that Angela will not feel unwelcome before she has had a chance to settle at the school (as you have experienced can happen). You really believe that things could start to settle for Angela in her new placement and that this could be successful if other things can just fall into place with the school.

Designated teacher

You are very committed to your role as DT but sometimes do not find you have the support of other senior staff and are under a lot of pressure resulting from league tables and other statistics. You have heard views about 'problem kids' being 'dumped' at your school in the staffroom. You have some good ideas about how to help Angela settle into the school and to reach her potential but you often find that external pressures on children in public care are greater than your efforts.

　　　　　　　　　　© John Holland and Catherine Randerson 2005

Carer

You feel that Angela is beginning to settle with you. However, she has experienced a lot of change and a lot of loss and rejection and you know it will take a long time for you to gain her trust. A big concern for you is that Angela gets settled in school and progresses academically, also that she quickly establishes some friendships. You feel quite anxious about the meeting and hope that it will prove to be a fresh start and that people will not have preconceived ideas about Angela and her experiences.

Mentor

You are looking forward to meeting Angela but are a little worried by what you have heard about her temper outbursts and how she will relate to you. You hope that plans will be made today to support you as well as Angela in making this school transition go smoothly. You are aware of Angela's special needs but hope to provide her with some space and time to explore things, feelings, worries, etc. As Angela's case is complex you are considering a request to go on some further training to help you do this.

You feel that proper plans made today will mean Angela has a good chance to settle in and do well, but have found in the past that people don't always work as a team in these cases.

Handout 15: Personal Education Plans (PEPs)

A Personal Education Plan (PEP) is a document that contains educational targets for a young person. A first PEP meeting should be held within 20 days of a child being admitted to the school, and must be made for every child in public care who is attending nursery or is of statutory school age. The PEP meeting is arranged by the young person's social worker, although the participation of carers and school (designated teacher) is very important. Others that may attend include the parent, Connexions staff, special educational needs co-ordinator (SENCO), class teacher, head of year, child protection co-ordinator, special educational needs support service, educational welfare officer (EWO), educational psychologist (EP), fostering social worker, and health staff.

The PEP is the vehicle by which expectations are raised and the achievements of the young person are recognised. It also gives an opportunity for the young person to be involved in the planning of his or her education.

The PEP gives the opportunity for the involvement of all the relevant agencies that could help to support the young person to be involved in the planning stage. A PEP needs to include details of the young person and of all those from the agencies supporting him or her. It needs to be completed quickly when a young person either becomes 'looked after' or changes school, and needs to be regularly reviewed to keep it as an active document.

A pupil profile could include details of the current placement, previous educational history and details of previous PEPs. Both short-term and long-term targets should be included with links to other documents, such as an Individual Education Plan (IEP) or Care Plan. Details need to be given of who is responsible to action the targets.

The PEP could also include a record of the young person's attainments, providing a history of his or her school achievements. The young person needs to be actively involved in the PEP.

17

'Jargon busting'

Introduction

A common difficulty in any field is the use of language or 'jargon' specific to that area. For those familiar with this language it often becomes used automatically and can become difficult for others to understand or else easily misunderstood. The research revealed that both teachers and carers, at times, had difficulty with jargon as shown on Transparency 43.

Aim

The outcome of this section is to explain the meanings of some common words, phrases and abbreviations used in relation to young people in public care, social work, health and education. Although it is not exhaustive it will, we hope, be a useful resource for course members and their colleagues.

Method of delivery

This section may be presented or simply its reason explained briefly and the handout provided to the course members.

Transparency 43 may be shown; these are the researched views of designated teachers and carers about technical words. Course members may then wish to share some experiences of their own in relation to this issue. Handout 16 can then be given out.

Are technical words confusing?

	DT	Carers
Yes	0%	52%
No	47%	27%
Sometimes	53%	21%

DTs: found 'technical' words used by other agencies confusing

Carers: found educational 'technical' words (PEP; IEP) confusing

Handout 16: 'Jargon busting'

Care Order (see Section 31 of the Children Act 1989)   Gives local authority parental responsibility (this may be shared), lasts until the young person is 18.

Designated Teacher (DT)   The teacher at the school who has overall responsibility for young people who are in public care. Each school should appoint one.

EPO (Emergency Protection Order) (Section 44)   Short-term order which allows the local authority to remove the child from (or prevent being removed to) a situation of apprehended danger.

Exclusions   The pupil is not allowed to attend the school, generally in response to serious behavioural difficulties relating to adults or young people at school. Either fixed-term or permanent. Only a total of 45 days within a school year are allowed for fixed-term exclusions.

Individual Education Plan (IEP)   A plan drawn up to support a child with identified Special Educational Needs at school.

Interim Care Order (see Section 38 of the Children Act 1989)   May be granted before a Care Order is granted whilst the evidence is considered. Contact rights are as in the full Care Order.

Key Stages   There are four key stages in the education system.

   Key Stage 1: refers to Years 1 and 2, i.e. pupils aged 5–7.

   Key Stage 2: refers to Years 3, 4, 5 and 6, i.e. pupils aged 7–11.

   Key Stage 3: refers to Years 7, 8 and 9, i.e. pupils aged 11–14.

   Key Stage 4: refers to Years 10 and 11, i.e. pupils aged 14–16.

Parental Responsibility (PR) (see Section 3 of the Children Act 1989)   The rights, duties, powers, responsibility and authority of a parent over a young person. Birth mothers and married fathers automatically have PR.

Pastoral Support Plan (PSP)   A plan written for a young person who is at risk of permanent exclusions from school. The plan should include targets and give positive rewards as well as sanctions and involves the appropriate outside agencies.

Personal Education Plan (PEP)   A plan which is required for every child in public care.

Residence Order (see Section 8 of the Children Act 1989)   Relates to where a young person lives and cancels a Care Order.

Schedule 1 Offender Person convicted of an offence of a physical or sexual nature against a minor.

Section 7 (Report) Gives the courts power to request a report into the wellbeing of a child either from social services (where the concern is possible harm) or the Children and Family Court Advisory and Support Service, or CAFCASS (where concern is post-separation conflict between parents). Hence the term 'Section 7 report'.

Section 17 Covers the duty to safeguard and promote the wellbeing of a child. Hence the terms 'S.17 money' and 'S.17 provision'. A local authority may not get a Care Order if it cannot evidence previous efforts to support the family through S.17.

Section 20 Child looked after voluntarily (with no court order) by a friend or family other than those regarded as unable to care for the young person.

Section 34/4 Court order for no contact is sought when a local authority does not wish a young person to have contact with those regarded as unable to care for him or her.

Section 37 (Report) Gives the court power to request a report from social services to indicate whether a Care or Supervision Order would be appropriate as a means of meeting a child's needs. Hence the term 'S.37 report'.

Section 47 Places a duty on the local authority to investigate allegations or concerns about possible significant harm to a child. Hence the term 'Section 47 inquiry' and/or 'investigation'.

Special Educational Needs (SEN) The educational needs of children at school over and above the 'normal response' of the school in terms of learning or other needs such as behaviour. There is a phased response and at a high level of need the child may have a 'Statement of Special Educational Needs', a legal document relating to their learning or behavioural needs at school.

Special Educational Needs Co-ordinator (SENCO) The teacher at the school who co-ordinates special needs.

Standard Assessment Tests (SATs) External assessments that take place at the end of Key Stages 1, 2 and 3 during May each year.

Supervision Order (see Section 31 of the Children Act 1989) Requires a 'responsible person', i.e. who has PR or with whom they live, to take reasonable steps to ensure compliance of the young person with a supervision order. Requires a supervisor to advise, assist and befriend the young person.

Further reading

Department for Education and Skills (1989) *Children Act.* London: HMSO.

Department for Education and Skills (2004) *Every Child Matters: Change for Children.* London: HMSO.

Department for Education and Skills (2004) *Every Child Matters: Next Steps.* London: HMSO. In a series of cross-agency publications. www.everychildmatters.gov.uk

Fletcher, B. (1998) *The Education of Children who are Looked After by Local Authorities.* London: The Who Cares? Trust.

Goldman, L. (1999) *Life and Loss.* London: Accelerated Development.

Granot, T. (2004) *Without You – Children and Young People Growing up with Loss and its Effects.* London: Jessica Kingsley Publishers.

Holland, J., Dance, R., MacManus, N. and Stitt, C. (2005) *Lost for Words.* London: Jessica Kingsley Publishers.

Klass, D., Silverman, P.R. and Nickman, S.L. (1996) *Continuing Bonds, New Understandings of Grief.* London: Taylor and Francis.

Kübler-Ross, E. (1970) *On Death and Dying.* London: Routledge.

Lacher, D., Nichols, T. and May, J. (2005) *Connecting with Kids Through Stories: Using Narratives to Facilitate Attachment in Adopted Children.* London: Jessica Kingsley Publishers.

Laverty, H. and Reet, M. (2001) *Planning Care for Children in Respite Settings: Hello, This is Me.* London: Jessica Kingsley Publishers.

Leaman, O. (1995) *Compassionate Approaches.* London: Cassel.

McParlin, P. (1996) *Education of Young People Looked After Pack.* Leeds: First Key.

Plummer, D. (2004) *Helping Adolescents and Adults Build Self-Esteem.* London: Jessica Kingsley Publishers.

Rose, R. and Philpot, T. (2004) *The Child's Own Story: Life Story Work with Traumatized Children.* London: Jessica Kingsley Publishers.

Social Inclusion Unit (2003) *A Better Education for Children in Care.* London: Office of the Deputy Prime Minister.

Staniford, P. (1996) *Improving Educational Opportunities for Looked After Young People – A Good Practice Guide for Resident Social Workers.* London: National Children's Bureau.

Staniford, P. (1999) *Personal Education Plan for Children and Young People in Public Care.* London: National Children's Bureau.

Tew, J. (2005) *Social Perspectives in Mental Health: Developing Social Models to Understand and Work with Mental Distress.* London: Jessica Kingsley Publishers.

Wheal, A. (2000) *The Foster Carer's Handbook. Second Edition.* Lyme Regis: Russell House.

Worden, J.W. (1991) *Grief Counselling and Grief Therapy.* London: Routledge.